EGYPT

MAJOR WORLD NATIONS
EGYPT

Frances Wilkins

CHELSEA HOUSE PUBLISHERS
Philadelphia

Chelsea House Publishers

3 5 7 9 8 6 4 2

Library of Congress Cataloging-in-Publication Data

Wilkens, Frances.
Egypt / Frances Wilkens.
p. cm. — (Major world nations)
Includes index.
Summary: Describes the history, geography, economy, culture, and
people of the North African nation of Egypt.
ISBN 0-7910-4989-2 (hc)
1. Egypt—Juvenile literature. [1. Egypt.] I. Title.
II. Series.
DT49.W55 1998
962—dc21   98-15075
CIP
AC

ACKNOWLEDGEMENTS

The Author and Publishers are grateful to the following organizations and individuals
for permission to reproduce illustrations in this book:
Rev. J.C. Allen; The Ashmolean Museum; Douglas Dickins; The Egyptian Embassy
Press Office; The Egyptian Ministry of Tourism; Shell Photographic Service; Alec
Spencer; UNICEF and WHO.

4

CONTENTS

Map		6 and 7
Facts at a Glance		8
History at a Glance		10
Chapter 1	The Land and the People	15
Chapter 2	Ancient Egypt	21
Chpater 3	The Pyramids	28
Chapter 4	The Treasure of Tutankhamen	33
Chapter 5	Later Times	39
Chapter 6	Egypt Today	44
Chapter 7	Islam	50
Chapter 8	Schools and Colleges	56
Chapter 9	The City-Dwellers	62
Chapter 10	Cairo and Alexandria	68
Chapter 11	The Nile	75
Chapter 12	The Fellahin	81
Chapter 13	The Deserts	89
Chapter 14	The Suez Canal	94
Chapter 15	Egypt in the Modern World	98
Glossary		100
Index		101

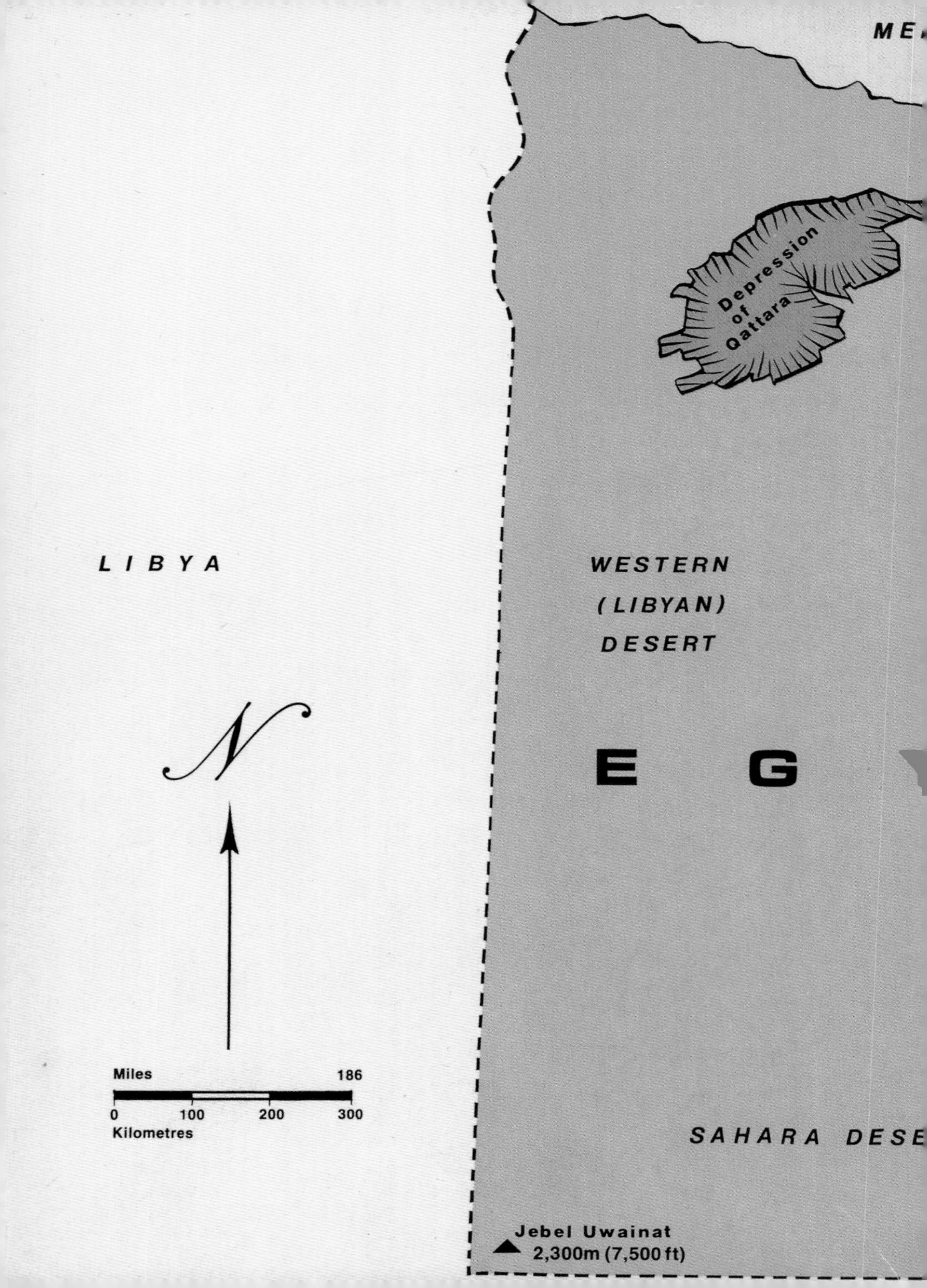

ME

Depression
of
Qattara

LIBYA

WESTERN
(LIBYAN)
DESERT

E   G

N

Miles   186
0   100   200   300
Kilometres

SAHARA DESE

▲ Jebel Uwainat
2,300m (7,500 ft)

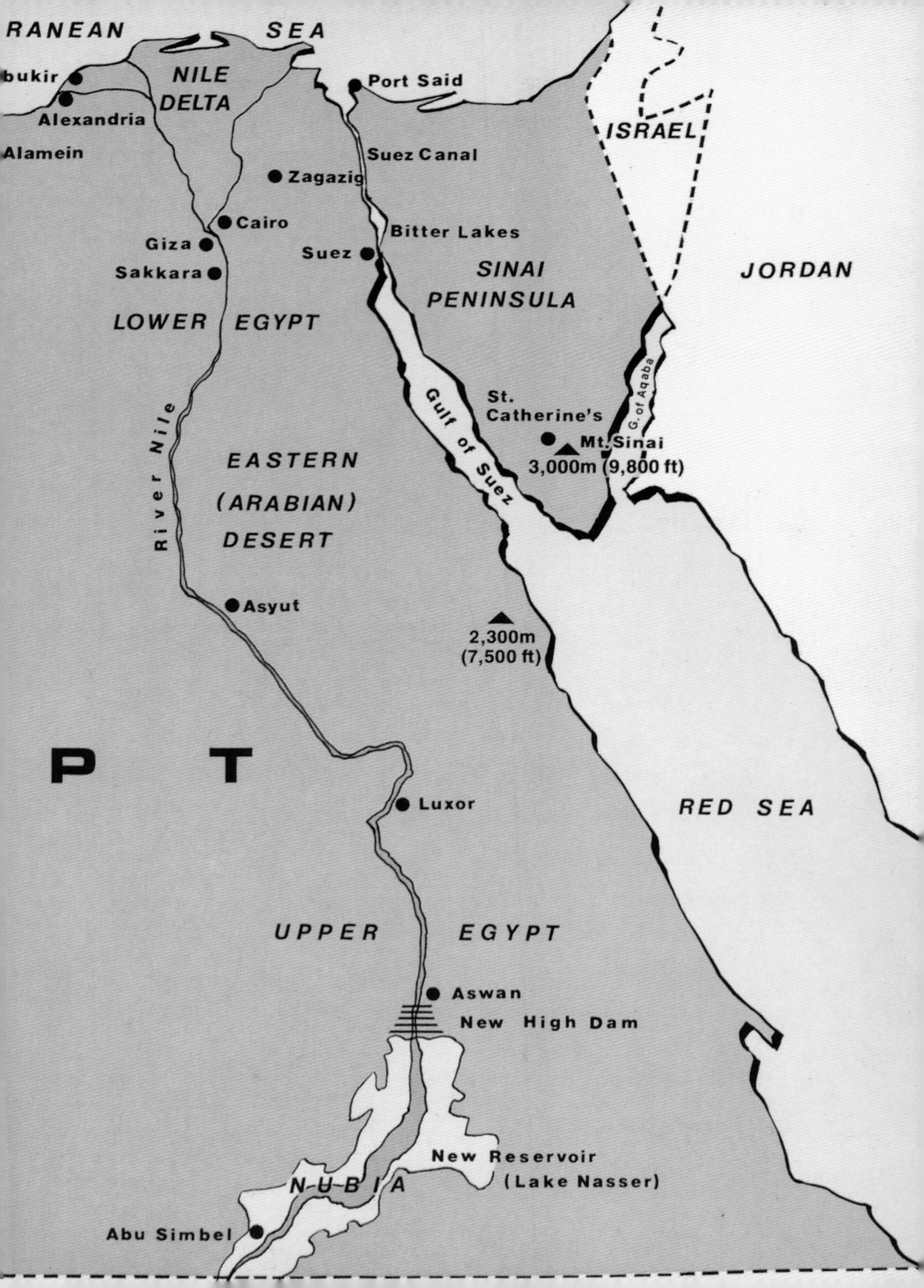
RANEAN
SEA
NILE
DELTA
bukir
Alexandria
Alamein
Port Said
ISRAEL
Suez Canal
Zagazig
Cairo
Giza
Sakkara
Bitter Lakes
Suez
SINAI
PENINSULA
JORDAN
LOWER
EGYPT
Gulf of Suez
G. of Aqaba
St.
Catherine's
Mt. Sinai
3,000m (9,800 ft)
River Nile
EASTERN
(ARABIAN)
DESERT
Asyut
2,300m
(7,500 ft)
P
T
Luxor
RED SEA
UPPER
EGYPT
Aswan
New High Dam
New Reservoir
(Lake Nasser)
NUBIA
Abu Simbel

FACTS AT A GLANCE

Land and People

Official Name	The Arab Republic of Egypt
Location	Located at the northeastern corner of the African continent and the southeastern end of the Mediterranean Sea
Area	385,227 square miles (997,738 square kilometers)
Climate	Hot and dry most of the year, except during the months of December, January and February
Capital	Cairo
Other Cities	Alexandria, Al-Jizah
Population	60 million
Population Density	161 persons per square mile (62 persons per square kilometer)
Major Rivers	Nile
Highest Point	Mount St. Catherine (Gebel Katherina) (8690 feet /2642 meters)
Official Language	Arabic

8

Religions	Muslims, Copts
Literacy Rate	50 percent
Average Life Expectancy	65 years for males; 69 years for females

Economy

Natural Resources	Iron ore, chromium, maganese
Agricultural Products	Cotton, wheat, rice, sugarcane, maize
Other Products	Livestock
Industries	Tourism, mining, manufacturing
Major Imports	Machinery, transport equipment, food, iron and steel products, chemicals
Major Exports	Petroleum, cotton yarn, textiles, basic metals
Currency	Egyptian pound

Government

Form of Government	Republic
Government Bodies	One legislative house (People's Assembly)
Formal Head of State	President
Head of Government	Prime Minister

HISTORY AT A GLANCE

3100 B.C.	Menes (or Narmer), first recorded pharoah, unites kingdoms of Upper and Lower Egypt.
2600-2000 B.C.	The Old Kingdom. Building of the pyramids.
2000-1600 B.C.	The Middle Kingdom.
1800-1600 B.C.	The Hyksos, a Semitic people, conquer Egypt.
1600-1580 B.C.	Egyptian rebels drive out the Hyksos and found the New Kingdom.
1470-1450 B.C.	Egypt reaches its height as a world power.
1370 B.C.	The pharoah Ikhnaton attempts to replace the gods of Egypt with the worship of one god.
1200 B.C.	Exodus of foreign slave laborers, who return to their former home in what is now Israel.
1100 B.C.	End of Egyptian Empire after the reign of Ramses III.
525 B.C.	Egypt conquered by the Persians. Egypt remains under foreign rule for 2,500 years.
332 B.C.	Alexander the Great occupies Egypt without opposition and he founds the city of Alexandria.

304 B.C.	After the death of Alexander his empire is divided among his generals. The descendants of the general Ptolemy rule Egypt for several centuries.
30 B.C.	In the civil war after the death of Julius Caesar, Roman forces enter Egypt. Cleopatra, the last of the Ptolemies, commits suicide after being defeated in battle.
639-642 A.D.	The Arabic general Omar conquers Egypt as part of the spread of Islam. A small Christian community survives, but Egypt becomes part of the Muslim world.
661	Egypt becomes part of the Umayyad Muslim dynasty, headquartered in Damascus. Umayyads are replaced by the Baghdad-based Abbasid dynasty (750).
1169-1193	The Seljuks, a Turkish people, become the dominant Muslim force in the Middle East.
1250	The Mamelukes establish independent rule in Egypt and Syria.
1517-1519	The Ottomans add Egypt to the last of the great Muslim empires. The Ottomans remain in control until World War I.
1799	Scientists accompanying Napoleon's expedition discover the Rosetta Stone, which enables the writings of ancient Egypt to be translated.
1805-1849	The reign of Muhammed Ali.
1869	The Suez Canal is completed.
1882	Nationalists under Araby Pasha seize the Suez Canal. British troops defeat the local forces. A

British-controlled Egyptian state, still officially part of the Ottoman Empire, is set up, which also administers the Sudan.

1914-1918 After Turkey enters World War I on the side of Germany, Britain occupies Egypt.

1924 The British government grants independence.

1940 With the outbreak of World War II, the British re-occupy Egypt.

1942 German forces advancing on the Suez Canal are defeated by the British at El Alamein, one of the decisive battles of the war.

1948-1952 Egypt opposes the formation of an independent Israel, but is defeated (1948-1949). The resulting discontent encourages army officers to overthrow the corrupt monarchy and begin modernizing the country.

1954 Gamal Abd-al Nasser emerges as the leader of the new military government. He begins an ambitious campaign to modernize Egypt.

1956 Nasser nationalizes the Suez Canal. Britain, France and Israel occupy the Canal Zone, but withdraw after diplomatic efforts by the United States and the then Soviet Union.

1958-1961 Egypt and Syria combine to form the United Arab Republic. Syria soon withdraws but Egypt continues to use the UAR title for some time.

1967 Israeli forces occupy the oil-rich Sinai territory after defeating Egypt in the Six-Day War.

1973 Egypt launches a surprise attack in an attempt to re-occupy the Sinai. The Egyptian army is unsuccessful.

1979 Egypt, now led by Anwar Sadat, signs a peace agreement with Israel at Camp David in the United States. This is part of a process that includes the re-opening of the Suez Canal and the withdrawal of the Israelis from the Sinai.

1981 Anwar Sadat is assassinated by Muslim militants.

1988 Cairo native Naguib Mahfouz wins the Nobel Prize for Literature.

1991 Egypt sides with the coalition against Iraq after the invasion of Kuwait. The U.S. forgives 14 billion dollars in debts owed by Egypt. Foreign investment increases.

A felucca on the Nile River.

1

The Land and the People

Egypt lies at the northeast corner of the African continent, at the southeastern end of the Mediterranean Sea. It is roughly square in shape, and covers an area of approximately 386,000 square miles (1,000,000 square kilometers). This means that it is more

Planting and tending crops in the delta region.

than four times the size of the British Isles.

When we look at a map, Egypt appears to be a large country. But little more than three percent of the land is fertile enough to be habitable. As a result, almost the whole population of more than sixty million people is crowded into an area of approximately 12,000 square miles (1,000 square kilometers).

This fertile area is a narrow strip along the banks of the Nile River. In southern (or Upper) Egypt this strip is less than half a mile (one kilometer) wide. It later broadens out to about 7 to 10 miles (12 to 16 kilometers), and then in northern (or Lower) Egypt it fans out to form the famous Nile Delta.

This large, triangular-shaped delta region is very fertile indeed. Virtually anything will grow there, from cotton and rice to potatoes, tomatoes and sugarcane. In fact, its fine, silt-like soil enables the farmers to harvest two, or even three, separate crops during the course of one year.

All the important cities of Egypt are also situated around the delta. In the south, just before the river begins to fan out, there is the capital, Cairo. At the tip of one of the western arms of the delta is the country's most important port, Alexandria; and near the tip of one of the eastern arms is the second largest seaport, Port Said.

Apart from the area around the Nile, Egypt is almost totally arid. In fact, the southern part of the country forms part of the vast North African desert—the Sahara. Where there is an oasis (a spring of water) there is usually a small town or village, but these are very few and far between, especially in the south of the country.

The climate of Egypt varies considerably from one region to another. Along the Mediterranean coast and in the Nile Delta the weather is generally temperate all year round. The summers are warm and dry, with an average temperature of about 65 degrees Fahrenheit (18 degrees Celsius). The winters are cool and wet, especially near the sea.

In the desert areas, however, the weather is totally different. In the hottest months, from May to October, the temperature often reaches 113 degrees Fahrenheit (45 degrees Celsius) or more, in the shade. Even in winter the midday temperature rarely drops below 68 degrees Fahrenheit (20 degrees Celsius). And, on average, there is only one rainy day in each year.

The great majority of the people who live in Egypt are Arabs. They are a distinct nation, however, and they differ in many ways from Arabs in other countries. Despite the fact that they have often

A Nubian woman.

been overrun by other nations, they have always managed to preserve their own special identity.

The only other sizeable racial group in Egypt are the Nubians. They live on the fertile banks of the Nile River, in the south of the country. The Nubians are of mixed Arab and Negro blood. They are mostly very dark-skinned and considerably taller than the Arabs.

The official language of Egypt is Arabic. It is a semitic language, which means that it is similar to Aramaic, the language spoken by Jesus. The Arabic spoken in Egypt is slightly different from the language spoken in the rest of the Arab world, but written Arabic is exactly the same in Egypt as everywhere else. There are twenty-eight characters in the Arabic alphabet, and it is written from right to left. To Western eyes, written Arabic looks rather like a graceful kind of shorthand. The Nubians speak their own language, which is called Kensi. It is a soft, sing-song tongue, with a great many of the words ending in vowels.

About ninety percent of Egyptians are Muslims. This includes the Nubians, who are renowned for being particularly pious. Muslims are the followers of the religious teacher named Muhammad, who was born in Mecca, a town in the Arabian peninsula, in the sixth century A.D.

Muhammad never claimed that he was god. He merely said that he was God's prophet, and that God had revealed certain truths to him. The most important of these truths was that there was only one God, called Allah, who was the creator of the entire universe, and that everyone should worship him.

18

A kerosene salesman. His cart advertises his wares in Arabic and English! The Arabic is written from right to left.

The name "Muslims" means "people who submit to God's will." Whatever happens to them, good or bad, the Muslims always accept it as being the will of Allah. It is sometimes said that this is why the Arabs are slow to improve their way of life. They feel it is useless to make plans when it is Allah who will decide the course of events.

19

A Coptic church in the old part of Cairo.

As well as the Muslims, about 10 percent of the population are Christian Arabs living in Egypt. Nearly all of them are members of the ancient Coptic Church. Most of them live by the Nile in the central part of Egypt. In fact, in Asyut and the villages round about they form the bulk of the population. They mostly work on the land, and in general are very poor. There are also quite a number of Copts living in Cairo. Once again, most of them are extremely poor, although a few of them are educated, professional people who work as teachers, doctors or lawyers.

2

Ancient Egypt

People were living beside the Nile at least five thousand years before the birth of Christ. They are thought to have come from other parts of North Africa, and also from western Asia. There are no written records of this very early period but archaeologists have uncovered the sites of numerous prehistoric villages and cemeteries along the banks of the Nile.

The first written records date from about 3100 B.C. It was then that a king, probably called Menes, united the whole of both Upper and Lower Egypt. Menes was the first of a long line of pharaohs who ruled Egypt for nearly three thousand years. During that time there were thirty-one separate royal houses, or dynasties.

King Menes established his capital at Memphis, near modern Cairo. He probably thought this was a place of strategic importance, and it was not too far from the fertile land of the Nile Delta. He also set a pattern for all the later pharaohs by building himself a large tomb. He was buried in it with all his treasured possessions which he thought he might need in the after-life.

King Menes' tomb was a huge pile of sun-dried bricks. In fact, it

The Great Sphinx of Giza.

was much the same as all the tombs built by the pharaohs for the next four hundred years. But in 2700 B.C., at the beginning of what is called the Old Kingdom, the pharaohs began building colossal stone tombs instead, and it is these that are now the world-famous pyramids.

The pyramid-building period lasted for five centuries. It was a time of great prosperity for the Egyptians, when their civilization reached one of its highest peaks. Indeed, the very fact that they were able to build the pyramids at all shows what an extremely high standard they must have reached in mathematics and science.

This prosperous period was followed by a time of great unrest. Several different branches of the royal family were all struggling to seize the throne for themselves. Finally, in 2050 B.C., the country was reunited under princes from Thebes, a town about 400 miles (650 kilometers) south of Memphis. From then on Thebes, and not Memphis, was the capital.

This was the beginning of the period called the Middle Kingdom. At first all went well, but in about 1730 B.C. Egypt was attacked by some tribes called the Hyksos. With their weapons of bronze and their war-chariots (both unknown in Egypt at that time), the Hyksos quickly conquered the northern part of the country, although the southern part was still held by the pharaohs. In 1570 B.C., the pharaohs managed to drive the Hyksos out, and the country was united once again.

This was the beginning of the Early New Kingdom, as it is called, which was probably the most prosperous period in the whole history of Ancient Egypt. One of the best-known rulers of this time was Queen Hatshepsut. Although she was officially only a regent, she reigned with absolute power for more than twenty-five years. She was followed by Thutmoses III, who was a soldier. Within twenty years he had established an empire which stretched all the way from the banks of the Nile to the Euphrates.

The temple of Queen Hatshepsut.

This great Egyptian empire lasted for nearly a century. Trade flourished, and Thebes and Memphis became the political and cultural hubs of the world. In fact, it was at this period that most of the magnificent temples and palaces at Thebes, and at the nearby area known as Karnak, were constructed.

Then a new pharaoh named Amenhotep IV came to the throne. (Today he is chiefly remembered because his wife was the beautiful Queen Nefertiti.) Amenhotep was not interested in the empire, which quickly disintegrated. He was only interested in establishing the worship of one god, instead of the many gods which the Egyptians had always worshipped before.

The pharaohs of the New Kingdom still believed in life after death. But they no longer built huge pyramids as the pharaohs of

24

the Old Kingdom had done. Queen Hatshepsut built herself a magnificent temple in what is now called the Valley of the Tombs of the Kings, near Thebes. Most of her successors built smaller, rock-hewn tombs in the same valley.

In the Later New Kingdom (1300-1090 B.C.) Seti I regained most of the lost empire, and his son, Ramses II, constructed the now famous temples at Abu Simbel. At the end of this period, Egypt fell on difficult times again, and was conquered first by the Libyans and

Karnak—the temple of Amon.

then by the Assyrians from the Tigris valley.

In 525 B.C. the Persians forced the Assyrians out of Egypt. They then took control of the country themselves and ruled it for nearly two hundred years. Finally, in 332 B.C., the famous Macedonian leader, Alexander the Great, conquered Egypt. After his death, it passed into the hands of one of his generals, named Ptolemy.

King Ptolemy and his successors ruled Egypt for nearly three centuries. During this time the court was Greek (both in language and culture) but the way of life of the ordinary Egyptian barely altered at all. In fact, it was a time of great prosperity for Egypt, particularly for Alexandria (the capital under the Ptolemies), which

A temple carving showing Queen Cleopatra and her son.

became one of the greatest centers of learning in the world.

The last of the Ptolemies was Queen Cleopatra. She became queen in 69 B.C., but only managed to retain her throne by marrying the Roman general, Mark Antony. A few years later they were both defeated by another Roman general at the Battle of Actium; and, in the following year, 30 B.C., Cleopatra ended her life by her own hand.

3

The Pyramids

In ancient times people used to speak of the Seven Wonders of the World. Today only one of these seven great wonders still exists. The last remaining wonder is the famous group of pyramids at Giza. They stand about 7 miles (11 kilometers) south of the center of modern Cairo.

The pyramids at Giza are by no means the only pyramids in Egypt. There are at least seventy others, all built sometime between 2700 and 2200 B.C. Some of the older ones, like the pyramid at Sakkara, are "step" pyramids. In other words, their sides do not slope smoothly and gradually upwards, but go up in steps.

To most people, however, the word "pyramids" means the three great pyramids at Giza. The largest of these was built by King Cheops, in about 2500 B.C. Its height today is nearly 164 yards (150 meters) but it was originally about 36 feet (10 meters) higher. The width of each side at the base is about 270 yards (250 meters).

Even today the Great Pyramid is very awe-inspiring. But when it was first built it must also have been extremely beautiful, as it was completely faced with white limestone. Since this limestone was the best building material available, when the Arabs came to Egypt in the Middle Ages they stripped all the pyramids of their outer surfaces, and used the stone to build mosques.

People have always been puzzled to know how the pyramids were constructed. The Great Pyramid alone is composed of over two million blocks of stone, each weighing something between two and fifteen tons. This is enough stone to build a wall more than 10 feet (3 meters) high stretching for over 3,000 miles (5,000 kilometers), or all the way from London to New York.

Most of the stone blocks were quarried locally and so did not have to be carried far. But the fine limestone for the outer casing came from Tura, about 16 miles (25 kilometers) further up the Nile. The real problem, however, must have been transporting the huge slabs of granite for the king's burial chamber, inside the pyramid. The nine slabs that form the ceiling weigh nearly four hundred tons altogether, and came all the way from Aswan, 500 miles (800 kilometers) to the south.

Almost certainly all the stone was transported by river. In fact, it was probably brought up the Nile in large, flatbottomed barges, while the river was flooding. During this period (approximately June to September) the waters of the Nile almost reached the edge of the site at Giza where the Great Pyramid was to be erected.

The summer months would also have been the best time for obtaining labor. No agricultural work could be done while the river was flooding, so there were always plenty of men standing idle. According to the Greek writer, Herodotus, one hundred thousand men worked on the Great Pyramid at a time. Even if this is an

The names and titles of Ramses II (in the pictorial writing used by the ancient Egyptians) together with a list of the offerings which were buried with him.

exaggeration, there must certainly have been a great army of workers.

Once the stone reached Giza, the problem of construction had to be resolved. Nowadays, most scholars believe that the stones were dragged up enormous earthen ramps to be placed in position. This seems the only possible method that could have been employed, as the Egyptians had nothing but sledges and wooden rollers to help them. (Even the wheel had not yet been invented.)

Despite all the difficulties, every pyramid was planned to be built in one lifetime. They were each erected by a different Egyptian king, who intended the pyramid to be his last resting-place. What was more, the pyramids did not stand alone. They were originally each part of a large burial complex, which usually included two temples, joined to the pyramid by a causeway.

When a king died, seventy days were spent on embalming the body. Then it was wrapped in long linen bandages, and became what is known as a mummy. The mummified body was taken, probably by river, to the first temple, where special prayers were said. Then it was carried along the causeway to the second temple. Finally, the body was taken into the burial chamber inside the pyramid itself. There, it was hoped, the royal body would rest in peace for all eternity. At the same time, it was believed that the royal spirit would ascend to join the sun-god in heaven, since the pharaohs were not regarded as ordinary mortal people, but as special, divine beings.

Unfortunately, none of the dead kings was allowed to rest in peace for very long. People who knew that there was treasure inside the pyramids were determined to get it. Despite the fact that all the entrances had been ingeniously concealed, robbers broke into all the pyramids in remote antiquity, and stole anything of any value.

Today, thousands of tourists flock to Giza from all over the world. They ride round the pyramids on camels, and some of them even climb to the top of the Great Pyramid itself. It is also possible to explore the interior of the Great Pyramid, although it means a great deal of climbing and stooping, and the air is rather stuffy and stale. If people want to go in, they first have to climb a little way up the

31

outside of the pyramid. Then they go through a small door, and climb an extremely long flight of stairs to the king's burial chamber. There is nothing in the chamber except the king's empty sarcophagus (stone coffin). Tourists can also visit the queen's burial chamber, which lies about 50 feet (15 meters) below that of the king.

Not far from the pyramids at Giza is the famous Sphinx. This has the body of a lion and the head of a king, although the face is now badly mutilated. It was carved out of one colossal piece of stone, which was considered useless for building purposes, during the reign of King Chephren. To give some idea of its size, its total length is about 260 feet (80 meters) each ear is 5 feet (1.5 meters) long and its mouth is nearly 8 feet (2.5 meters) wide. Thousands of other sphinxes were built in Ancient Egypt. A great many can still be seen today, but none of the others is as large as the one at Giza.

4

The Treasure of Tutankhamen

The greatest tourist attraction in Egypt is undoubtedly the pyramids. A very close second is the area around the modern town of Luxor, about 400 miles (650 kilometers) south of Cairo. This was the site of the ancient city of Thebes, which was the capital of Egypt during one of the most flourishing periods in its history.

On the eastern bank of the Nile at Thebes stood the famous Temple of Karnak. This was dedicated to the great god Amon-Ra, and numerous pharaohs added new statues and obelisks to it. Eventually it became the largest temple the world has ever seen, occupying a site that would have held three of the largest European cathedrals—St. Peter's in Rome, Milan Cathedral and Notre Dame in Paris.

On the opposite bank of the river was the Valley of the Tombs of the Kings, dominated by the gigantic temple of Queen Hatshepsut, with all its broad terraces and magnificent colonnades. There were also numerous other royal tombs in the Valley, all cut straight out of the living rock, roughly between 1570 and 1085 B.C.

The tomb of Ramses VI in the Valley of the Kings. The tomb of Tutankhamen is nearby.

The pharaohs hoped that these tombs cut out of the rock might not be plundered as the pyramids had been. In fact, they were all robbed of their treasures soon after they were constructed. At least all the tombs discovered up to the beginning of this century had been robbed. At that time, there was one man, an English

34

Ram-headed sphinxes at Karnak.

archaeologist named Howard Carter, who felt certain that there was still one more tomb to be found.

For several years Carter dug in the Valley without success. Then, in November, 1922, his workmen uncovered the top of a short flight of steps. In great excitement Carter cleared the rest of the sand away. There, just as he had hoped, he found the entrance to what was clearly a royal tomb. What was more, the seals on the door showed that this was the tomb Carter was looking for. It was the burial place of a young king called Tutankhamen, who had died in about 1330 B.C.

Carter carefully made a small hole in one corner of the door. Then, holding up a candle, he strained his eyes to peer through the tiny aperture into the darkness beyond.

"Can you see anything?" asked his friend, Lord Carnarvon, anxiously.

35

"Yes, wonderful things," replied Carter. And wonderful things they most certainly were. Carter was gazing in the flickering candlelight into a room piled high with priceless articles of dazzling beauty and exquisite workmanship.

The first objects to catch his eye were three great gilded couches. On these couches, and all around, there were gold chests and caskets, alabaster vases, gold inlaid stools and countless other treasures. There were also some of the articles that the young king must have used when he was alive—the little chair he sat on as a child, his musical instruments and his golden chariots as well as several boxes of food. One of the most valuable and fascinating items in the tomb was a solid gold throne. In fact, many scholars consider it the most beautiful object that has ever been found in Egypt. A panel in the back, studded with silver and precious stones, portrayed the young king seated on a chair in his garden, while his elegant young queen anointed his shoulder with perfume.

In all this bewildering array of treasure the most important item was missing, however. This was the actual sarcophagus of King Tutankhamen. At first, Carter thought it must have been stolen. Then he noticed a door almost completely covered with plaster, and guarded by two tall wooden figures. Its meaning was clear. He was only in an anteroom. The place where the long-dead king still lay was beyond that mysterious door. So, as soon as he had sorted out all the objects in the anteroom, Carter made a small hole in this hidden entrance, and shone his torch through.

Even he was not prepared for what he then saw. There appeared to be a wall of solid gold, stretching in either direction as far as he

The two wooden figures guarding the door to the burial chamber of Tutankhamen's tomb.

could see. It was, in fact, the side of an immense gilt shrine, 18 feet (5.5 meters) by 11½ feet (3.5 meters), and nearly 10 feet (3 meters) high.

This was only the beginning of Carter's discoveries. Inside this shrine there was another, then another, and then yet another shrine of the same kind. Finally, the fourth shrine was opened to reveal a huge quartzite sarcophagus, guarded at each corner by the statue of a goddess, stretching her arms protectively over it. When the sarcophagus was opened it seemed to contain just a shrouded human figure. But as the shrouds were slowly pulled away, Carter could only gasp with amazement. For there, filling the entire sarcophagus, lay a magnificent gilded and jewelled coffin, carved in the likeness of the eighteen-year old King Tutankhamen.

There were two of these gilded coffins, one inside the other. But when Carter reached a third coffin he found that it was made of solid gold. No man in modern times had ever seen a sight to compare with it.

Carter slowly opened the wonderful gold coffin to see what lay inside. The slight human figure which was the cause of all this magnificence was wrapped in blackened pieces of linen, but they were adorned with so many precious ornaments that the body itself could hardly be seen.

Most impressive of all was the mask of beaten gold, fitted over the head and shoulders, which was fashioned in the likeness of the king, and which seemed to glow with a light of its own.

Today, all the fabulous treasures from the tomb of King Tutankhamen can be seen in the Cairo Museum—including the famous mask, which is the largest solid gold object in the world. All, that is, except the body of the boy king. This was carefully examined and then taken back to sleep peacefully once more in the Valley of the Kings.

5

Later Times

The story of Egypt from the time of Cleopatra's death right up to modern times is the story of one foreign invasion after another. Nation after nation coveted the fertile land of the Nile Valley, or thought that Egypt would make a useful link for them between Europe and the East.

The first of these many conquerors were the Romans. Almost immediately after Cleopatra's death they overran the whole of the country. Then they and their successors, the Byzantines, ruled Egypt for more than six hundred years. It was during this period that many of the Egyptians became Christians, and founded the Coptic Church.

In A.D. 639, the Arabs invaded Egypt. They first captured Alexandria, and then quickly conquered all the rest of the country. For the next two hundred years Egypt remained part of the vast Arab empire. Under the influence of the Arabs, during this time, most of the Egyptians renounced Christianity and became Muslims.

The next invaders were another group of Arabs, called the Fatemites. They came from Tunisia in A.D. 969, and soon gained control of the whole of Egypt. They decided to build a new capital (which they called Cairo) a short distance away from Memphis, the original capital.

During the Crusades, the Arab caliph (or ruler) of Egypt asked the Sultan of Syria, another Muslim country, to help him defeat the Christians. The Sultan duly sent a general called Saladin who, instead of helping the caliph, overthrew him and took control of Egypt for himself.

Saladin's successors continued to rule Egypt until A.D. 1250. Then the Mamelukes (Turkish slaves who had been the royal bodyguard) revolted and seized power. Nearly three hundred years

The Muhammad Ali mosque in Cairo—the city built by the Fatemite invaders of Egypt.

later, the Turks themselves conquered Egypt; for almost another three centuries Egypt formed part of the great (Turkish) Ottoman Empire.

The Mamelukes were still in charge of the day-to-day administration of the country, however, and as time went on they became increasingly harsh and oppressive. This gave the great French general, Napoleon, just the excuse he needed for interfering in Egyptian affairs to his own advantage.

In 1798, Napoleon invaded Egypt with a force of forty thousand men. He said he had come as a friend of the Turkish sultan to end the repressive rule of the Mamelukes. His true objective, however, was to cut Britain's vital link with the East, and so make it easier for France to attack Britain.

Much to his surprise, however, the Egyptians did not welcome Napoleon. Apparently they thought that even life under the Mamelukes was preferable to being ruled by the French. As a result, Napoleon had to force his way to Cairo, with no help from the Egyptians, while the sultan's representative in Egypt hastily returned to his own country for advice.

Meanwhile, the British, under Admiral Nelson, were searching for the French fleet. They found it lying at anchor just off Abukir, and quickly destroyed it. This was the end of Napoleon's dreams, as his supply lines were now cut. A year later, the British invaded Egypt and forced him to withdraw.

The Turks for their part had also turned against Napoleon. In fact, they had even engaged a group of Albanians to help them drive the French out of the country. This, oddly enough, led to a totally unexpected development taking place in Egypt's history, for the leader of the Albanians was a remarkable man called Muhammad Ali.

It was soon clear that Muhammad Ali was an outstanding administrator. Immediately after the fighting was over he was asked to stay in Egypt, to help rebuild the ruined country. This was no easy task, as the country was little more than a devastated battlefield. But Muhammad Ali succeeded so well that he was named the new ruler of Egypt, an honor and responsibility which was later to pass to his descendants.

In 1875, the British became the owners of the newly opened Suez Canal; and, in order to protect their interests they decided to send a garrison there. Within a few years there was so much restlessness in Egypt, however, that the garrison no longer seemed adequate, and the British decided to take control of the whole country.

The British Protectorate, as it was called, lasted until 1922, by which time the British thought that the country was sufficiently stable to be independent again. So Egypt became a kingdom, still ruled by the descendants of Muhammad Ali. The first ruler of this kingdom was King Fuad. The second, who succeeded his father in 1936, was King Farouk.

During the Second World War, both Germany and Italy invaded Egypt. Like Napoleon, they wanted to break Britain's vitally important links with the East. The British resisted and, after much bitter fighting at a place called El Alamein, both the Germans and the Italians withdrew.

In 1951, rebellion broke out in Egypt. The chief reason for the revolt was that people thought Farouk's government was corrupt, and not really concerned with the good of the nation. The Egyptians were also angered by the fact that a mere handful of wealthy aristocrats owned practically all the agricultural land in the country, while the farm-workers themselves were paid barely enough to keep themselves alive. In addition, there was considerable bad feeling towards the king himself. People knew that Farouk lived a life of riotous luxury while many of his subjects were starving. So, in July 1952, a group of army officers seized control of the government. And King Farouk, his family and friends were forced to go into exile.

6

Egypt Today

The abdication of King Farouk marked the end of an era. In fact, the modern history of Egypt is generally considered to have begun in 1952. Nevertheless, several events had already taken place a few years earlier which were to have very important and far-reaching effects on the country's future.

The first of these events took place in 1947, when the United Nations agreed to establish a Jewish state, to be called Israel, on the northeastern side of the Sinai peninsula. Egypt immediately invaded Israel, on the grounds that the whole of the Middle East belonged to the Arabs, but two years later they decided (for strategic reasons) to withdraw.

Egypt was still determined to bring Israel to her knees, however. So, in 1950, the Egyptians closed the Suez Canal to all Israeli ships, and fighting quickly broke out again. The Egyptians were no luckier this time than they had been before, however, and this was one more reason for the unpopularity of Farouk's government, and for the king's eventual downfall.

When the army seized power, the new government was at first

A view across the desert.

headed by General Neguib. He was quickly superseded, however, by another soldier, Colonel Gamal Abdul Nasser. For the first eleven months, Farouk's infant son was (in name) the Head of State. But in 1953 Egypt was formally declared a republic.

The new regime was popular with practically all the Egyptians. It was the first time in history that the country was not being ruled by a pharaoh, a king or a foreigner. Nasser further increased his popularity by persuading the British Government to withdraw (by June 1956) the last of their troops, who were still guarding the Suez Canal.

Nasser then turned his attention to building a huge new dam across the Nile. This was absolutely essential, he declared, for Egypt's future prosperity. At first Britain and the United States offered to help. Later, they decided that Egypt did not have sufficient resources to make the scheme a profitable venture, and they withdrew.

Nasser retaliated by seizing the Suez Canal from its British and French owners. Then he proclaimed that all the tolls from the canal would in future be used to build the new dam. Russia then took the opportunity to strengthen her position in the Middle East by offering to supply all the men and materials that Egypt would need.

All through the nineteen-fifties Nasser's popularity continued to grow. All over the Arab world, and not merely in Egypt, people regarded him as the greatest man of the time. They believed that he would free the Middle East from all Western influence and control, and also destroy their hated enemies—the Israelis. Nasser was so

A view of Aswan.

popular, in fact, that in 1958 he even persuaded Syria to merge with Egypt to form the United Arab Republic with himself as the first president. His hope that all the other Arab nations would also become part of the new republic was never realized. Only three years later, Syria herself withdrew from the alliance.

In 1967 Nasser turned his thoughts towards Israel again. He massed his troops in the Sinai peninsula, and began making preparations for another invasion. But, on June 5th, while the Egyptians were still mobilizing, the Israelis themselves invaded the Sinai Desert, and in one massive strike destroyed almost the entire Egyptian air force. The Egyptians fought back for six days but, even with the help of Syria and Jordan there was clearly nothing they could do against the Israelis. When the Six-Day War was over, the Israelis were in occupation of the whole Sinai peninsula and, in retaliation the Egyptians closed the Suez Canal to all shipping.

After this defeat, Nasser offered to resign as president. But the Egyptians still had faith in him; they insisted that he stay on as their leader. From that time onward he was really a broken man. When he died, in September, 1970, most of his dreams and ambitions were still unfulfilled. Nevertheless, the whole Arab world mourned Nasser's death. He had been a great leader, and he had given the Arabs some idea of what they might one day achieve. Today, his name still lives on. It is commemorated by the lake that was formed by the building of the new High Dam at Aswan. It is called Lake Nasser, and is the largest man-made stretch of water in the world.

Nasser was succeeded as president by Anwar el-Sadat. Like Nasser himself, Sadat was one of the army officers who had forced

King Farouk to abdicate. Eleven years later, however, in October 1981, President Sadat was assassinated and was succeeded by President Hosni Mubarak, who remained in power through the 1980s and 1990s.

Today Egypt calls herself "a democratic, socialist state." Her aims are officially stated as: Arab unity, freedom for everyone and socialism. The first aim, Arab unity, was brought just a little closer in April 1982 when Israel agreed to withdraw her troops from the Sinai peninsula, and it came under Egyptian administration once again.

Mubarak has maintained peace with Israel, while loosening the political reins of a limited democracy. In 1991, he sided with the Allies in the Persian Gulf War against Iraq.

The biggest problem remaining is the rise of Islamic fundamentalist violence. Hundreds of people were killed between 1992 and 1995 in internal fighting. Since a number of those killed were tourists, the government has waged campaigns to assure the world of Egypt's safety.

In 1992, special laws were introduced in order to sentence to death alleged terrorists. By 1995, most of the death sentences were carried out.

In 1995, an unsuccessful attempt was made to assassinate Mubarak while on a visit to Addis Ababa, Ethiopia. Later that year, the Egyptian embassy in Islamabad was bombed. Violence persists and in 1996 there were sixteen Greek tourists massacred in Cairo.

In Egypt, the President alone is responsible for choosing the Prime Minister and the Council of Ministers (equivalent to the

British Cabinet), and he also has the power to dismiss them.

The National Assembly, which has 360 members, and sits for a five-year term, is democratically elected, but again the President can dismiss them whenever he chooses.

For the purposes of local government, Egypt is divided into twenty-five provinces. Each of them is administered by a local council under the advice and guidance of a governor. At the moment, these councils are only responsible for such matters as education, employment and health, but the hope is that eventually they will form part of what has been described as "a truly socialist, co-operative society."

7

Islam

Muhammad (the founder of the Muslim religion) was born in Mecca in about A.D. 570. At the age of forty he believed he had seen a vision of the Archangel Gabriel. The angel told Muhammad that there was only one God, called Allah, and that Allah had chosen Muhammad to be his prophet and to tell everyone about the new faith.

Muhammad gradually gathered a small band of followers around him. But their numbers increased so slowly that he finally decided

A Muslim saying his prayers.

The Al-Azhar Mosque in Cairo.

to leave Mecca and go to Medina. This was a town about 155 miles (250 kilometers) to the north. To Muhammad's delight, the people there received him with great enthusiasm. He then decided to spread the new religion by force of arms. He told his followers that every drop of blood they shed was equivalent to two months spent in prayer. Within a few years, almost the entire Arab world had embraced Islam—as the new faith was called—and long before the end of the seventh century A.D. Egypt had also become a Muslim country.

The Muslim equivalent to the Bible is the Koran. It is a collection of the sayings of Muhammad, which Muslims believe were inspired directly by God. The sayings were collected together by some of Muhammad's friends about a year after his death. They give the Muslims instructions on almost every aspect of their lives.

Islam differs from most religions in having no specially trained

51

ministers. The *khatib* (who preaches to the people) and the *imam* (who leads the prayers) are just ordinary men. They are chosen for their piety and learning, but they are not granted any particular privileges. Most of them spend only a few hours a week on their religious duties, and do some other kind of work the rest of the time.

Muslim places of worship are known as mosques. They usually have a dome, and a slender tower called a minaret, with a crescent on top. Mosques are usually built from the whitest stone that can be found, such as marble. In Cairo, quite a number of mosques are built from the white limestone which used to cover the pyramids. Before entering a mosque, people must take off their shoes or cover them with canvas slippers. This is done partly out of reverence and partly to keep the dust of the streets out of the mosques. Muslims are also expected to wash their face, hands and feet before they enter. In the courtyard of every mosque there is a fountain, or a tank of clean water, where this can be done.

To Christians, the interior of a mosque often seems empty and uninteresting. Usually the only furniture is an elaborately carved pulpit, with steps leading up from the front. There are no seats or benches. The floor is generally covered with thick, soft rugs. The Muslims kneel down and touch the ground with their foreheads over and over again as they pray. Christians also notice the absence of pictures and statues. These are never seen in a mosque, or anywhere else in the Muslim world, for that matter. Muslims believe that it is wrong to try to copy living things. This is the reason why all Arab decoration consists of geometrical designs, or is based on Arabic writing.

For a Muslim, the most important feature of a mosque is the *mihrab*. This is a tall, arched recess in one of the walls, usually close to the pulpit. When Muslims pray they always look towards the *mihrab*, and then they know they are looking towards Mecca. It is one of the commandments of their religion that they must always face the Prophet's birthplace when they pray.

Every day of the week Muslims are supposed to face Mecca five times and pray at dawn, at midday, in the afternoon, at sunset and after dark. They sometimes go to the mosque to say these prayers, but it is not uncommon to see them unrolling their prayer-mats at home, at work or even at the side of the road. When it is time for prayer, an official called a *muezzin*, cries out in a loud voice, "Allah is most great! I testify that there is no god but Allah! Come to prayer! Come to salvation!"

At one time the *muezzin* used to climb up to a small balcony at the top of the minaret to call the faithful, but nowadays the voice of the *muezzin* is generally recorded, and is just relayed from the minaret.

The Muslims' holy day, equivalent to the Christian Sunday, is Friday. Most of the shops and factories are closed, so that the faithful can go to the mosque. Both men and women attend the services, but the women have to sit either on a balcony or in a special area downstairs, partitioned off from the main part of the mosque.

One month every year is known to the Muslims as Ramadan. It is a time, rather like Lent, when they try to purify their lives and draw closer to God. During Ramadan Muslims may neither eat nor

53

drink while it is daylight. Officially, daylight begins as soon as it is possible to tell a white thread from a black one, and ends when the two threads can no longer be told apart. As the Muslim calendar is a lunar one (based on the phases of the moon), Ramadan falls ten days earlier each year. It is exacting even when it falls in winter, but it must require tremendous devotion and self-denial to go without even the least sip of water the whole of a long, scorching day in summer. Nevertheless, all strict Muslims, both men and women, observe the fast faithfully. When it is over, everyone celebrates with a holiday lasting three days, called *Id al-Saghir*.

Numerous other holy days are celebrated by the Muslims with feasting and jollity. One of the most important is Muhammad's birthday, when almost every Egyptian town has its own fair or carnival. There are wheels of fortune, merry-go-rounds and even dodg'em cars, and when it grows dark there are huge firework displays on the banks of the Nile.

As well as praying regularly, every Muslim tries to visit Mecca at least once in his lifetime. When he has done so, he is entitled to call himself a *hajj*, or a pilgrim. During the pilgrimage he must wear a robe with no seams in it and he must not cut his hair or shave. He must also do no harm to any living thing, not even an insect or a plant.

8

Schools and Colleges

A familiar sound all over Egypt used to be a high-pitched chanting. It told everyone within earshot that there was a Koranic school not far away. There are still some of these old schools, particularly in the villages, each under the supervision of the local mosque, but they are fast giving way to modern, Western-style schools.

Only boys attended the Koranic schools. They would squat cross-legged on the ground in a circle around the teacher. They had no books, but they usually balanced a small board on their knees and wrote on these boards with a reed pen, dipped in a thin ink made from burnt wool and water.

The method of teaching did not vary for centuries. The teacher read a verse from the Koran, and the boys repeated it over and over again, swaying backwards and forwards all the time. Then the boys wrote the verses down on their boards. Any boy who had not learned all the verses by heart by the end of the day was likely to get a beating.

Occasionally a few other subjects, such as math, were also taught at a Koranic school. But how much the boys learned chiefly depended on how much the teacher himself happened to know! The boys usually only went to school a few hours a day, and never on Fridays. On Thursdays, they made some small payment to the teacher, either in money or in kind. For centuries, the Koranic schools were the only schools in Egypt. As a result, the vast majority of the people remained almost completely illiterate. Even during the days of the British Protectorate there was little improvement. The British built schools for their own children, but did practically nothing for the children of the native population.

Then, in 1925, the first move was made to raise educational standards. The Egyptian Ministry of Education announced a plan for free, compulsory education on Western lines for all the children in the country. It was, however, obviously going to be a considerable time before the plan was fully implemented. There were no school buildings, no teachers and no textbooks except at the most elementary level. In fact, little or nothing had been achieved by the time Egypt became independent. As soon as General Neguib took office he made a bold promise. Every day, for the following ten years, work would begin on a new school somewhere. It was a promise which proved impossible to keep, but at least it showed that education was at last recognized as being of vital importance.

Today, 97 percent of Egypt's children attend school regularly. They begin when they are six years old, and they remain in the primary department for six years. This completes the compulsory period of education at the present time, but some of the children go on to spend three years at a lower secondary school and possibly

Both boys and girls wear school smocks, even when they are as small as this.

another three years at a higher secondary school.

In the first class in the primary schools the children concentrate on reading and writing. In the second class they begin arithmetic, using Egyptian figures. In both classes they also spend some time on practical subjects. The girls usually learn cooking, and the boys are taught some useful craft such as brickmaking.

When they reach the third class the children begin learning some science. They also start studying the Koran, but they do not have to learn long passages by heart as Egyptian children did in the old days. By the time they reach the third class, the pupils also spend much more time on practical work. The girls learn sewing and

58

Egyptian children start school at six years old—these children are in a kindergarten.

embroidery, and the boys often study farming.

In the fifth year two new subjects are added to the curriculum. One is the study of Egyptian history, and what might broadly be described as current affairs. The other new subject is a foreign language. Most Egyptian children, when they have a choice, choose to learn English, but quite a number of them choose French, German or Russian.

In primary schools there are several periods a week of gymnastics. This includes all kinds of exercises and routines as well as movement to music. Each year the best groups of children from schools all over the country go to Cairo to take part in a special celebration to mark Independence Day.

Only a small proportion of Egyptian children go on to secondary schools. Although the secondary schools are free, just like the primary schools, pupils are only accepted if they have reached a certain academic standard. The syllabus is closely modelled on the curriculum in Western schools, and it includes regular periods devoted to sports. The most popular sports are soccer, tennis, basketball, volleyball and swimming.

There has been a university in Cairo ever since A.D. 972. It is the famous Al-Azhar University, and today it is regarded as the "Mother University" of the entire Muslim world. It has more than twenty thousand students from all over North Africa and Asia. Apart from the Al-Azhar, there are five other universities in Egypt. Two of the most important are at Giza (just outside Cairo) and at Alexandria. In all these new universities the education is roughly the same as in Europe. There are faculties in all the usual subjects, and degrees are awarded after courses lasting from three to six years.

Boys being trained to do metalwork.

Egyptian women now follow a number of professions. This rural nurse has been carefully trained to help and advise village mothers.

It was recently decided to conduct most of the lectures in English at these universities. This means that students can now use up-to-date textbooks which are not available in Arabic. There was some opposition to the decision, as Arabic is regarded as a holy language (being the language of the Koran), but the change is now generally accepted as being essential, especially for medicine and science.

Another important step forward has been the admission of women. There is now, on average, one woman student for every four men in all the modern universities in Egypt. As a result, women are at last able to follow professional careers, if they wish to do so. Already there is a growing number of women in medicine, law, teaching and commerce.

9

The City-Dwellers

Nearly all Egyptians with high incomes live in the cities. Most of them work in factories or offices, or are professional people, such as doctors and lawyers. In many cases their wives also go out to work, especially if they are young and well-educated, just as women do in most Western countries nowadays.

The majority of the city-dwellers live in flats, usually in blocks of five or six stories. Nearly all the flats have balconies, where people can sit out when the weather is not too hot. Only the very poorest people live in the center of the cities. The more wealthy people prefer to live in the suburbs, and travel to work by bus or train every day. The apartments are usually furnished in much the same way as an apartments in Europe. People buy their furniture on a rent to buy basis, and like to have all the latest electrical appliances and gadgets. There are usually electric fans in each room to keep people cool, but an increasing number of well-to-do Egyptians are now having modern air-conditioning installed.

Most businesses in Egypt open at seven or eight o'clock in the morning. To make up for this early start, there is a long lunch break–from about one o'clock to about five or six o'clock in the afternoon. During the lunch break everyone goes home for the main meal of the day. There is also time for a short sleep, or at least a rest, before returning to work. Businesses close in the evening at about seven or eight o'clock. Most people then have a fairly light meal, and get ready to go out for a stroll. It is so hot in Egypt for most of the year that no one wants to go out in the middle of the day, but by the time evening comes they are longing for a breath of fresh air. After their stroll the Egyptians sometimes go to a movie. The programs do not begin until nine or ten o'clock at night, but people do not feel tired, as they have all had a rest in the middle of the day. What they like best, though, is to spend their evenings with friends and relatives, as they are an extremely hospitable people and they love being together in a happy, noisy group.

Sometimes Egyptians watch television in the evening, or play their radios or record-players. (Popular Western tunes and

A market scene. Fresh fruit and vegetables are always on sale.

traditional Eastern music arc equally enjoyed.) While they are relaxing, they often sip sweet black coffee or drink mint tea. If they are strict Muslims they never drink wines or spirits, as these are strictly forbidden by the Muslim religion.

Egyptian housewives probably spend much more time cooking than most Western women do. The midday meal, in particular, is regarded as a social event, to be planned and prepared with great care. It usually starts with an assortment of smoked sardines, various chopped meats served in tiny rolls, stuffed eggs and some beans served in olive oil. This is generally followed by meat served with some kind of rice. Yellow saffron rice topped with boiled lamb is very popular; so are stuffed vine leaves and rice. Whatever the food, the Egyptians like it to be highly seasoned. They use a great variety of pungent herbs and spices in preparing all their meat and fish dishes.

The meal ends with fresh fruit or some very sweet little cakes. There are also plenty of hot, newly baked loaves of bread if anyone is still hungry.

Children usually drink *laban* which is made from ass's or goat's yogurt diluted with water and flavored with salt. The adults drink root beer with their meals. They also drink tea and *sherbet*, a very sweet drink made from diluted fruit juices.

On festival days and national holidays the food is even more elaborate. All the family is at home all day, and so they have plenty of time to sit round the table and enjoy themselves. Nowadays, the most important festival is July 23rd. This is Independence Day (Revolution Day), and marks the overthrow of King Farouk by a group of army officers in 1952.

As can be seen from this view of Cairo, many of Egypt's city dwellers live in modern homes.

Most of the other holidays are connected with the Muslim religion. One of the most popular is the spring festival, called "The Scent of the Breeze"—in Arabic, *Sham an-Nesim*. According to the ancient Egyptian calendar, this was the day the world was made. To the Muslims, it represents the coming of spring and the earth's rebirth after the winter. Most city families like to spend *Sham an-Nesim* in the open air. All the parks and gardens are filled with people strolling in the sunshine, and with happy, laughing children. Most of the families take with them picnic baskets filled with hard-boiled eggs, fish and fruit. They then return home for an enormous meal in the evening.

65

Most Egyptian city-dwellers today wear Western clothes. But some strict Muslim women still cover themselves from head to foot in a black *melaya* every time they go out. They wear this voluminous, long garment even if they are only going out for a car ride. But the moment they return home they change into Western clothes.

As well as the more affluent people, there are also some extremely poor people in the cities. They live in mud huts or in broken-down shacks, without any kind of modern conveniences. Many of them are Copts, who can usually be distinguished by the blue cross which they have tattooed on the backs of their hands as a sign that they are Christians.

If they are lucky, these poor people have some kind of job. The very poorest may be boot-boys, for example, as all they need for this is a brush and a piece of rag. If they are not quite so poor, they may have a small portable charcoal stove from which they sell roasted corn-on-the-cob.

The old and the crippled are often forced to be beggars, however. They sit or squat on the pavement, crying out plaintively, "Alms, for the love of Allah! Alms, for the love of Allah!" They know that it is strictly laid down in the Koran that all Muslims must help the poor. They hope that by calling on Allah's name they will remind people of their duty.

A Cairo street scene.

10

Cairo and Alexandria

The capital of Egypt is the city of Cairo. It was founded in A.D.969 by the Muslim invaders called the Fatemites. Today, it has a population of more than sixteen million; it is the largest city not only in Africa but in the entire Arab world.

The Cairo Tower.

68

Liberation Square, Cairo.

The only high ground around Cairo is the Mokattam Hills. From the slopes of these hills there is a panoramic view over the whole of the city. For centuries this just meant the area between the hills and the Nile River, but today the city also covers a large amount of land on the further bank of the river.

Half way up the hillside is the famous Cairo Citadel. This was built in A.D. 1177 by the Great Saracen leader, Saladin. Also on the slopes of the Mokattam Hills is the Muhammad Ali Mosque. It is named after the nineteenth-century ruler of Egypt, who is buried there. Although the mosque is Turkish rather than Egyptian in

69

The main bridge across the Nile in Cairo.

appearance, with its cluster of domes and two very tall, thin minarets, it used to be the best-known landmark in Cairo. Nowadays, however, the best-known landmark is the Cairo Tower, which stands on Gezira (one of the two islands in the Nile). This striking monument was built for telecommunications and is 460 feet (140 meters) high.

One of the most fascinating places in Cairo is the Khan el-Khalil Bazaar. It is a maze of narrow, twisting lanes, crammed on either side with small stalls and open-fronted shops. The owners of some of these shops are Turks, Syrians or Armenians. They can often be seen busily working in a back room, making the goods they are offering for sale.

All the shops selling the same kind of articles are grouped

70

Feluccas—traditional Arab sailing-boats.

together in the bazaar. For instance, there are alleys full of silversmiths; and others with nothing but carpet-sellers. Other alleys are filled with the pungent smell of Eastern spices, and yet others with the curious, rather heady smell of exotic Egyptian perfumes.

On the edge of the Khan el-Khalil lies the famous Al-Azhar Mosque. This was originally built by the Fatemites more than a thousand years ago, but it has been altered many times over the centuries. Attached to it is the old Cairo University. Although it teaches little but Koranic studies, the University still has an enormous prestige, and the students are very proud of their grey caftans and turbans.

The heart of Cairo today, however, is Liberation Square. This is the spot where the ancient civilizations of Asia and Africa and that of the modern Western world meet. Above the tall blocks of offices there are neon signs urging people to fly to America with Egyptair, while on the pavement below there are beggars covered with sores, sleeping on filthy pieces of matting. There are men in long striped caftans and the traditional red fez walking only a few paces away from women dressed in the latest Paris fashions. Huge American automobiles sweep past slow, horse-drawn wagons (piled high with watermelons or sugarcane) or even past an occasional camel cart.

Not far from Liberation Square is the main bridge across the Nile. The huge carved stone lions at either end were erected during the British Protectorate. The bridge crosses to the island of Gezira, where people with time to spare often sit in one of the open-air cafes, and watch the *feluccas* (the traditional small Arab sailing-boats with two masts) sailing up and down the Nile.

The Mahmudiya Canal, near Alexandria.

At the southern end of the other island, Roda, stands the famous Nileometer. This is a pillar fixed in a well with markings to measure the rise and fall of the river. In ancient times when the river fell below eighteen cubits people knew that they must irrigate the land; if it rose above twenty-four cubits then they were warned of a flood. A cubit is roughly 19 inches (50 centimeters).

In recent years Cairo has become an important industrial center. Cotton is now made into cloth there, instead of being sent to Britain for manufacture. There are large steel-works, several car factories and some food processing plants. And most of the films which are shown in movie theaters all over the Arab world are made in Cairo.

The second city of Egypt is Alexandria. It was founded by Alexander the Great in 332 B.C., and when he died he was buried there. For the next three hundred years, under the Ptolomies, Alexandria was not only the capitol of Egypt, but also a world-famous center of culture and learning.

During the reign of Ptolomy I a great library was founded at Alexandria. It contained more than half a million different volumes, all written on papyrus. There was no other library like it anywhere in the ancient world. Unfortunately, it was destroyed by Christian fanatics in A.D. 391.

Also under the Ptolomies one of the very first lighthouses was built on an island called Pharos. This was just at the entrance to Alexandria's great harbor. According to writers of the time, the Pharos lighthouse was more than 400 feet (130 meters) high, and it was regarded as one of the Seven Wonders of the World.

Alexandria lost most of its glory after the Romans conquered

Alexandria is famous for its port. As the picture shows, it also has a popular beach.

Egypt. In fact, it was more or less neglected by all the various rulers of Egypt until the early nineteenth century. Then, in 1805, when Muhammad Ali took over the government he decided to rebuild the city, and also to construct a large naval dockyard there.

Today, the city of Alexandria has a population of more than five million. It is Egypt's chief port, and handles at least eighty percent of the country's exports and imports. It is also an important manufacturing center, with cotton processing and dyeing works, car factories, and all kinds of industries connected with transport.

11

The Nile

No country in the world is so dependent on a river as Egypt. In fact, Egypt has often been described as "the gift of the Nile." It is only the water from this mighty river that saves the country from being a complete desert, for Egypt has no more rain in a year than the United States might have in a single thunderstorm.

The Nile has done much more than merely provide Egypt with water, however. For centuries it has also been responsible for all the crops that have grown so abundantly in the Nile Valley. Every year, in about June, just when it would seem natural for a river flowing through hot, desert land to dry up, the Nile has always, very surprisingly, risen. By September it has usually been overflowing its banks. Then, in about December every year, the river has always gradually returned to its normal height once again. As it has gone down, however, it has left behind it a rich deposit of black mud. It is this that has made the land around the Nile one of the most fertile areas in the world.

In ancient times the Egyptians did not understand what made the Nile behave like this. They thought it must be the work of some

Farmland in the Nile Delta. Note how successive layers of silt have built up the fertile river bank.

wonderful river god. Today, however, we know that the Nile is the longest river in the world, and that it is due to geographical conditions far away in Ethiopia that the Nile rises and falls. The Nile has two sources. Every year, extremely heavy rainfall, combined with melting snow from the mountain tops, turns both the rivers into torrents. They then join together and rush down the hillsides with such force that they wash away millions of tons of rich topsoil, which is eventually deposited on the river banks in Egypt.

It has always been vital for the Egyptians that the river should

76

rise exactly the right amount. If it rose too little, not enough of the land was flooded, and the crops were very scarce. If it rose too much, on the other hand, the Egyptians knew that it would flood all the nearby villages, and that their homes were in danger of being washed away. For this reason, they have always tried hard to control the Nile. Even far back in antiquity they constructed primitive catch basins and dams. In fact, the very first pharaoh of all Egypt, King Menes, who lived in about 3100 B.C., launched very extensive irrigation and drainage projects.

It is only in modern times, however, that people have been able to harness the Nile effectively. To do this they needed to build a huge dam, right across the river from one side to the other. The first dam, finished in 1902, was 18½ miles (30 kilometers) long and nearly 100 feet (30 meters) high, but it still did not completely control the rise and fall of the river.

So in 1956 new plans were made to build an even larger dam. This was to be 4 miles (6 kilometers) upstream from Aswan, and was to form the largest man-made lake in the world. Egypt was not wealthy enough to build this dam by herself, however. Nor had she all the skilled technicians who would be needed for the immense, ten-year project. Both Great Britain and the United States offered to help but it was eventually the then Soviet Union which supplied all the money and other assistance which Egypt needed. Russia loaned Egypt the money for the project, supplied more than two thousand technicians, and also provided, on loan, enough equipment to move more than ten million tons of earth.

Money and skilled labor were not the only problems, however.

Egypt also had to find new places to live for thousands and thousands of people who were made homeless by the construction of the huge reservoir. These people were mainly Nubians, whose ancestors had generally lived in the same tiny villages for countless generations. They were eventually resettled in a place now named New Nubia, about 37 miles (60 kilometers) to the north.

Building the dam also threatened to drown many precious ancient relics. In particular, two of ancient Egypt's most famous temples would vanish forever beneath the lake. Both of them were situated at Abu Simbel, about 186 miles (300 kilometers) upstream from Aswan, and both were built during the reign of Ramses II, in about 1280 B.C.

When news spread about the destruction of the temples, people in more than fifty different countries, all over the world, sent money so that the temples could be moved to a new site. It was an incredibly difficult task. The Great Temple was 120 feet (37 meters) high and 186 miles (300 kilometers) wide. Even the Small Temple was 43 feet (13 meters) high and 98 feet (30 meters) wide. Nevertheless, every stone was carefully removed and numbered, and then gently lifted by a crane to a plateau about 230 feet (70 meters) above the old site. Then the laborious task of reassembling all the thousands of separate stones began. It took two thousand

Lake Nasser.

The Aswan High Dam.

men about seven years, and was an extremely expensive project.

The High Dam at Aswan has made a great change in the life of the Egyptians. The annual flooding of the land beside the Nile is now a thing of the past. The great reservoir behind the dam, called Lake Nasser, is almost the length of England. The water can be released exactly when, and in the exact quantities, required. This means that about one million acres more land can now be irrigated. It is calculated that, as a result, the Egyptian farmers have been able to grow almost twice the usual amount of crops. In addition, the dam produces over half the country's total electric power, including all the electricity that is used in the whole of Cairo.

12

The Fellahin

Nearly eighty percent of the people in Egypt are peasants who work on the land. They are called *fellahin,* and their way of life has not changed appreciably in the last four thousand years. They still employ much the same agricultural methods, live in much the same kind of homes, and are only slightly, if at all, better off than their long ago ancestors.

Water-carriers in an Egyptian village. Nearly eighty percent of the Egyptian population are peasants who work on the land and live in villages like this one.

An irrigation canal.

The only major change is that cotton is now their chief crop. It was introduced into Egypt on a large scale by the British (when the American Civil War cut off their usual source of supply). Egyptian cotton is of an exceptionally high quality, with extremely long fibers, and more than seventy percent of it is exported all over the world.

The next most important crops are wheat and rice. Watermelons, sugarcane, maize and beans are also grown almost everywhere in the Nile Valley. Most *fellahin* tend a few fruit trees, as well. The most common types are date palms, lemon and orange trees and mango trees.

The greatest problem facing the *fellahin* is still irrigation. Since the

82

construction of the new High Dam at Aswan they know they will always have exactly the right amount of water each year. But they still have to raise the water from the Nile, or from the thousands of small canals that run from it, up to their fields, which are always on a slightly higher level.

The most common way of raising the water is by using a *shadoof*. This is a kind of see-saw, with a bucket dangling from a rope at one end, and a weight at the other. When the bucket has been filled in the river, the weight makes it easy to lift. Then the water is poured

Using a shadoof to raise water.

A water-buffalo working a water-wheel.

into the ditches that run across the fields. Another method of raising water is by using a waterwheel. The little buckets on the wheel are filled in the river, and then spill their water out over the fields. The wheels are usually worked by a water-buffalo—a large-boned animal with a mud-colored coat and horns the shape of bicycle handles.

A few lucky *fellahin* have a diesel-pump to raise the water, but even today it is probably only one farm-worker in several hundred who is able to afford one. A pump costs more than most *fellahin* normally earn in two or three years, and they usually need all their earnings just to feed and clothe themselves and their families.

The *fellahin* always build their own houses. To make the bricks, they scoop up some mud from the river, add some chopped straw and then pour the mixture into brick-shaped wooden molds. They then leave the bricks to dry in the sun for several days. The roofs of their houses are usually thatched with straw or with sugarcane stalks.

There is very little furniture in the houses of the *fellahin*. There may be a few mattresses, a table and a few stools, but that is generally all. Perhaps this is just as well, as the family's water-

A typical Egyptian village.

Making mud bricks.

buffalo usually sleeps in the house at night, and it would soon smash to pieces any fragile furniture.

The staple food of the *fellahin* is rice. But beans are also extremely popular with most families. They are served hot or cold, alone or made into soups and stews. The fellahin also eat bread at nearly every meal. The bread in Egypt has no yeast in it, and the loaves look rather like thick, crusty pancakes.

The cooking is usually done over a charcoal fire. The food is placed in a large copper bowl or (more often than not) an old petrol can. As much cooking as possible is always done at one time, as fuel is very expensive in Egypt. There are no natural deposits of coal or oil, and virtually no timber either.

After the evening meal, the *fellahin* often meet their friends in a café. (The women are not allowed in these cafés, and have to meet in their own homes.) The men usually drink mint tea, and smoke a *hookah*—a special kind of pipe with a long tube which passes through a jar of cold water before it reaches the smoker's mouth.

As might be expected, the heat and the lack of any form of modern sanitation lead to all kinds of diseases being rife among the *fellahin*. One of the most common diseases is an infection of the eyes called trachoma. Another very widespread complaint is bilharzia, which robs the sufferer of all his energy. Bilharzia is particularly difficult to treat, because it is caused by a minute parasite which lives in the marshy waters of the Nile. Even if the patient is cured by modern drugs, the moment he goes back to work and stands

Farmers with their water-buffalo.

with bare feet in the muddy fields he is likely to contract the illness again.

There is one way, however, in which life has improved for the *fellahin* in modern times. They are no longer working for wealthy landowners who are only interested in making as much money as possible. When President Nasser took office in 1952 one of his first actions was to confiscate all the large estates, and break them up into numerous small plots. He then gave all these plots to the *fellahin* who worked on the land. For the first time in history they had become their own masters. Today, no individual in Egypt is allowed to own more than 198 acres (80 hectares); no one will ever be able to build up enormous estates again.

13

The Deserts

The Western, or Libyan, Desert covers more than twothirds of Egypt. It is part of the great Sahara, which stretches across the whole of North Africa. The Western Desert is, on average, about 650 feet (200 meters) above sea level, but in the extreme southwest the Jebel Uwainat mountains rise to nearly 7,500 feet (2,300 meters).

The Western Desert also possesses some deep depressions. The Qattara Depression, for example, is more than 325 feet (100 meters) below sea level. These depressions are always burning hot, even in winter, in much the same way as the peaks of mountains in other countries are sometimes snow-capped in summer.

The Eastern Desert, often called the Arabian Desert, is also part of the Sahara. From the Nile Valley it rises gradually to nearly 7,500 feet (2,300 meters) near the Red Sea. Numerous rocky valleys with steep sides, called *wadis*, which were originally cut by streams which have now dried up, also intersect nearly the whole of the Eastern Desert.

There is practically no vegetation at all in either of these deserts.

Camels are the beasts of burden for both Bedouin and fellahin. This is a familiar sight in many parts of Egypt.

This means that they are virtually uninhabitable, as there is no food, water or shade. The edge of the Eastern Desert, however, is the home of some nomads, known as Bedouin, who still live the same wandering life as their ancestors have lived for centuries. These Bedouin are a cheerful, carefree people. Although they usually own nothing except a camel, a tent and perhaps some tools or a rifle, they appear quite content. Efforts made by the government to settle them very rarely meet with success. Many of the Bedouin assist the desert patrols. They are regarded by the authorities as extremely useful and trustworthy.

The third desert region of Egypt is the Sinai Peninsula. This is a large, triangular-shaped piece of land. Geographically it belongs to

Asia and not to Africa. It is flanked on the western side by the Gulf of Suez and on the eastern side by the Gulf of Aqaba, both of which are arms of the Red Sea.

In many ways the Sinai Desert is much the same as any other arid part of the country. It is, however, much more mountainous than either the Western or the Eastern Desert. The whole of the southern end of the peninsula forms one vast plateau; in the extreme south some of the peaks rise to more than 10,000 feet (3,000 meter). These craggy mountains are both forbidding and strangely impressive. There are many different-colored veins in the rock which give them an unusual beauty. In the winter, the tops of the

A camel caravan—traditional means of transport in Egypt through the ages.

highest peaks are often snow-capped. In the rest of the peninsula, on the other hand, the weather is hot throughout the year.

There is also a little more vegetation in the Sinai Peninsula than in the other two deserts. Here and there can be found an oasis, where a tiny village has sprung up. These oases may be a considerable distance from each other, however, and very few, if any, have more than one hundred inhabitants. An oasis stands out in the desert on account of its tall date palms. These provide the people who live there with virtually everything they need. As a food, the dates are rich in fat, sugar and protein; the palm fibers, can be used to make ropes and matting, and the trunks provide the frames for the people's simple clay houses. The palms are also greatly valued for the shade they give. Figs, peaches, oranges, lemons and pomegranates can all be grown under their waving fronds. Yet more crops can be planted in the shade of the fruit trees. Wheat, barley, millet, pumpkins and tomatoes all grow well in the oases.

Although most of it is so barren, the Sinai peninsula has a trickle of visitors. They come because of Sinai's connection with a number of stories in the Old Testament. For example, when Moses was leading the Chosen People through the Wilderness in search of the Promised Land he was, according to the Bible, wandering through the Sinai Desert. It was also on Mount Sinai (one of the peaks in the mountain range in the south of the peninsula) that Moses received the Ten Commandments. There is one spot, in particular, that is regarded with special reverence in Sinai. This is the place where Moses is said to have seen the burning bush and heard the voice of

92

God speaking to him. This is also in the south of the peninsula, not far from Mount Sinai, and today it is the principal place of pilgrimage for Christians in modern Egypt.

As early as the fourth century A.D. there was a chapel on this spot. It was said to have been built by the Roman Empress St. Helena, and it was dedicated to Our Lady. Then in A.D. 527 the Roman Emperor Justinian erected a new chapel there, and also a monastery called St. Catherine's, which is now the modern name of this area.

The present monastery is occupied by a small community of monks of the Greek Orthodox church. It is a picturesque huddle of buildings of different shapes and sizes. There are monks' cells, a maze of passages, some small courtyards, an ancient well, some tiny gardens and, of course, a small church and a bell-tower.

From June 1967 to April 1982, the Sinai peninsula was occupied by the Israelis. But life continued exactly as before for most of the desert people. They still regarded the peninsula as one of the Egyptian provinces, and themselves as Egyptians and just waited patiently for the time to come when the Israeli troops would withdraw. Under the Camp David Agreement, Israel agreed to pull out in 1982.

14

The Suez Canal

Nearly two thousand years before the birth of Christ there was a canal joining the Red Sea to the Nile River. It is thought to have been dug in the reign of the pharaoh Sesostris I. It was probably still in use in the time of Seti I, who died in 1290 B.C., but soon afterwards drifting sands closed the outlets in the south to the Bitter Lakes.

When the Romans conquered Egypt they repaired the canal. For the next five hundred years it was one of the busiest stretches of water in the world. Merchants from all over the East sent their exotic merchandise—spices, fine fabrics and exquisite jewels—to Rome by way of the canal.

After the fall of Rome, no one in Europe wanted such luxuries. So the canal fell into disuse, and was soon choked with sand once again. From then on, anything brought from the East had to be carried on camels across the narrow isthmus, or else taken by sailing-ship around the southern tip of Africa.

By the late eighteenth century the greatest power in the East was Britain. But, oddly enough, the British Government showed no interest at all in reopening a short sea-route to the Orient. They apparently disliked the idea of paying tolls, and they also thought they might lay themselves open to all kinds of "interruptions, extortions and insults" if they made themselves dependent on a canal.

The French Government, on the other hand, took quite a different view. They believed that a canal would be invaluable in helping them to develop their trade with the Far East. So when Napoleon conquered Egypt in 1798 he ordered surveys to be carried out with a view to digging a canal directly from the Red Sea to the Mediterranean. Nothing came of the idea, because the British soon drove the French out of Egypt. But the French engineers did decide that a little Egyptian town called Suez would make an excellent harbor at the southern end of the canal. So Napoleon ordered that the water there should be deepened, and he even went as far as establishing a naval dockyard on the banks of the Red Sea.

Then, in 1854, a new name appears in the story of the canal. This was Ferdinand de Lesseps, who had originally come to Egypt as a member of the French Consular Service. De Lesseps was a close friend of the new ruler of Egypt, a man called Pasha (Governor) Said, and for many years they had talked together about the advantages of cutting a canal.

As soon as the Pasha came to power, de Lesseps thought that his chance had come. Although he was not an engineer, he drew up plans for a canal, and submitted them to the Pasha for his approval. The Pasha was delighted. He at once ordered a special company to be formed to put the work in hand, with de Lesseps, of course, as the company's first president.

De Lesseps hoped that the new company would be internationally financed. But Britain, the United States and Russia all stubbornly refused to give the project their support. As a result, when work eventually began in 1859, virtually all the shares were owned either by private individuals in France or else by the Egyptian Government.

The first task facing de Lesseps was to build a harbor at the northern end of the canal. This was no easy matter, as there was no drinking-water there, nor any of the other necessities of life. Nevertheless, the harbor was finished by 1860. De Lesseps named it Port Said, in honor of his old friend the Pasha.

Work then began on the Sweet Water Canal, as it was called. This was to bring fresh drinking water from a place called Zagazig to the new canal zone. Nearly seven thousand laborers were needed, as all the work had to be done by hand. But in less than two years the entire canal, more than 44 miles (70 kilometers) long, was completed.

It was then possible to begin cutting the Suez Canal itself. At first, all the work was still done by hand, and nearly twenty thousand laborers were employed. Later, however, when de Lesseps managed to obtain more financial backing, steam-operated dredgers, excavators and cranes were all brought from France.

It was a tremendous undertaking, especially for that period. But finally, on November 16, 1869, the Suez Canal was officially opened to shipping. It was 100 miles (160 kilometers) long, 55 to

96

110 yards (50 to 100 meters) wide on the surface, and on average nearly 30 feet (9 meters) deep.

By 1875, almost four-fifths of the ships using the Suez Canal were British. So when Benjamin Disraeli, the British Prime Minister, had the opportunity to buy it he leaped at the chance. Five years later, the British became concerned that their interests in the canal zone might be in danger, and British troops moved in. They were to remain in occupation until May, 1956.

By the time the British troops finally left, many changes had taken place. Nearly 275 million tons of shipping was using the canal every year. The canal had also been widened several times, so that it could accommodate the ever larger and larger ships which were being used to carry cargo.

In July, 1956, Colonel Nasser nationalized the Suez Canal. This meant that nearly all the British engineers who had been chiefly responsible for operating the canal had to leave. However, despite some fears to the contrary, the Egyptians managed to operate the canal themselves perfectly well, until it was closed for political reasons in 1967.

It was opened again in 1975, but some people now wonder if the Suez Canal is outdated. The huge, modern super-tankers are too large to pass through it, and a great deal of merchandise is now carried by air. Nevertheless there will probably always be some ships which want to travel quickly and easily from Europe to the East, or vice versa, and prefer to sail a mere 100 miles (160 kilometers) instead of 5,000 miles (8,500 kilometers).

15

Egypt in the Modern World

Everywhere in Egypt today there is the sound of transistor radios. They can be heard in the streets, in shops, on buses and in the parks. They are so cheap that almost everyone seems able to afford one; many young people carry them around with them wherever they go.

For this reason, the Egyptians today are well aware of what is going on in their country, as well as what is happening in many other parts of the world. What is more, the Egyptian government can easily inform people of its plans, and of what is required of them if Egypt is to become a vigorous, prosperous, up-to-date nation.

There are still some Egyptians, of course, who sigh for the old days. They still believe that the only education anyone needs is a knowledge of the Koran. These people are suspicious of any modern advances, because they feel that Egypt is an Arab state, and should not be influenced by the West, or by any other non-Arab countries, for that matter.

Most Egyptians today, however, believe that it is possible to learn from the rest of the world without in any way losing their own

A street scene typical of modern Egypt and the tall buildings of its big cities.

national identity. In fact, they know that without a knowledge of modern economics and technology they cannot possibly realize their full potential as a modern, independent nation.

President Sadat once said, "There are two phases in every revolution. First men lead the revolution, and then the revolution leads the men." For some Egyptians their country is being led just a little too quickly into the twenty-first century, but most of them are extremely proud of their independence and of their achievements.

99

GLOSSARY

Allah   The Islamic name for God.

Islam   Religion that follows the teachings of the prophet Muhammad who lived in the sixth century A.D.

Kensi   Language spoken by the Nubians.

Koran   Holy book of the Islamic religion similar to the Christian Bible.

Mecca   The holy city of the Islamic religion.

minaret   Tower in a mosque.

mosque   Place of worship in the Islamic religion.

Nubians   People of a racial mix of Black and Arab.

oasis   Green fertile area in the desert.

pharoah   Ancient Egyptian king.

pyramids   Large stone tombs built for the kings (pharoahs) in ancient Egypt.

Ramadan   A holy month of fasting and prayer in the Islamic religion.

sarcophagus   Carved and decorated stone coffin used in ancient Egypt.

INDEX

A

Abukir, 41
Abu Simbel, 25, 79
Actium (Battle of), 27
agriculture, 29, 75, 80, 81
Al-Azhar Mosque, 71
Al-Azhar University, 60
Albanians, 41-42
Alexander the Great, 10, 26, 73
Alexandria, 8, 10, 16, 26, 39, 60, 73-74
Allah, 18, 19, 50
Amenhotep IV, 24
Amon-Ra, 33
Arabian Desert, 89
Arabian Peninsula, 18
Arabic, 8, 18, 53
Arabs, 17, 18, 19, 20, 29, 39, 44, 47, 51, 98
Aramaic, 18
arid land, 16
Armenians, 70
Assyrians, 26
Aswan, 29, 47, 77, 79, 80, 83
Asyut, 20

B

Bedouin, 90
bilharzia, 87

Bitter Lakes, 94
British, 11-12, 16, 41, 45, 46, 57, 77, 82, 94-95, 96, 97
British Protectorate, 42, 57, 72, 73
burial chambers, 31, 32, 38
burning bush, 92
Byzantines, 39

C

Cairo, 8, 16, 21, 28, 33, 40, 41, 52, 68-73
Cairo Citadel, 69
Cairo Museum, 38
Cairo Tower, 70
Carnarvon, Lord, 35
carnivals, 55
Carter, Howard, 35-38
Cheops, King, 28
Chephren, King, 32
Christians, 11, 20, 39, 52, 66, 73, 93
Cleopatra, Queen, 11, 27, 39
climate, 8, 17, 90
clothes, 66
Copts, 9, 66
Coptic Church, 20, 39
cotton, 73, 82
Crusades, 40

D
dams, 47, 77-80
deserts, 89-93
Disraeli, Benjamin, 97

E
Early New Kingdom, 10, 23, 24
Eastern Desert, 89, 91
education, 56-61, 98
El Alamein, 12, 42
electricity, 80
embalming, 31
entertainment, 63, 73, 87
Ethiopia, 76
Euphrates River, 23

F
factories, 62, 73
Farouk, King, 42-43, 44, 48, 64
Fatemites, 39, 68, 77
fellahin, 81-88
feluccas, 72
fertile land, 16, 21, 75
festivals, 64-65
flooding, 29, 73, 77, 80
food, 64, 65, 86, 92
food processing, 73
foreign invasions, 10, 39
French, 12, 41, 46, 95
fruit trees, 82, 92
Fuad, King, 42

G
Germans, 12, 42
Gezira, 70, 72
Giza, 28-32, 60
Great Pyramid, 28, 32

Great Temple, 79
Greek Orthodox monks, 93
Gulf of Aqaba, 91
Gulf of Suez, 91

H
hajj, 55
Hatshepsut, Queen, 23, 25, 33
Helena, Saint, 93
High Dam, 80, 83
holy day, 53
hookahs, 87
housing, 62, 66, 81, 85
Hyksos, 10, 23

I
Id al-Saghir, 54
Ikhnaton, Pharoah, 10
imam, 52
Independence Day, 59, 64
industries, 9, 73, 74
Iraq, 13, 48
irrigation, 73, 77, 80, 82-83
Islam, 50-55
Israel, Israelis, 10, 12, 13, 44, 46, 48, 93
Italians, 42

J
Jebel Uwainat Mountains, 89
Jordan, 47
Justinian, Emperor, 93

K
Karnak, 24, 33
Kensi, 18
Khan el-Khalil Bazaar, 70-71
khatib, 52

Koran, 51, 56, 58, 98

L

Lake Nasser, 47, 80
Later New Kingdom, 25
Lesseps, Ferdinand de, 95-96
Liberation Square, Cairo, 71
Libyan Desert, 89
Libyans, 25
lighthouse, Pharos, 73
Lower Egypt, 10, 16, 21
Luxor, 33

M

Macedonians, 26
Mahfouz, Naquib, 13
Mamelukes, 40, 41
Mark Antony, 27
Mecca, 18, 50, 51, 53
Medina, 51
Mediterranean, 8, 15, 17, 95
melayas, 66
Memphis, 23, 24, 40
Menes, King, 10, 21, 77
Middle Kingdom, 10, 23
mihrabs, 53
minarets, 52, 68
Ministry of Education, 57
Mokattam Hills, 69
Moses, 92
mosques, 29, 52, 56
Mount Sinai, 92, 93
Mubarak, President Hosni, 48
muezzin, 53
Muhammad, 18, 50-51, 54
Muhammad Ali, 11, 42, 74
Muhammad Ali Mosque, 69

mummies, 31
Muslims, 9, 11, 18, 19, 39, 50-55, 64, 68

N

Nasser, Colonel, 12, 45, 46-47, 88, 97
National Assembly, 49
Nefertiti, Queen, 24
Neguib, General, 45, 57
Nelson, Admiral, 41
New Nubia, 78
Nile River, 8, 16, 21, 29, 55, 69, 75-80, 83, 94
Nile Delta, 16, 17, 21
Nileometer, 73
Nile Valley, 39, 75, 89
North Africa, 16, 21, 60
Nubians, 18, 78

O

Old Kingdom, 10, 22, 25
Old Testament, 92
Ottoman Empire, 11, 12, 41

P

Pasha, Araby, 11
Pasha Said, 95-96
Persian Gulf War, 48
Persians, 10, 26
pharaohs, 21, 22, 23, 24, 31, 33, 34, 45, 77, 94
Pharos, 73
Port Said, 16, 96
professions, 60-62
Ptolomies, 11, 26, 27, 73
Ptolemy, 11, 26, 73
pyramids, 10, 22, 24, 28, 29, 31, 33, 34, 52

Q
Qattara Depression, 89

R
Ramadan, 53
Ramses, 10, 25, 79
rebellions and revolutions, 42-43
Red Sea, 89, 91, 94, 95
religion, 9
Roda, 73
Romans, 39, 73, 94
Russia, 12, 46, 77, 96

S
Sadat, President Anwar, 13, 47, 48, 99
Sahara, 16, 89
Saladin, 40, 69
Saracens, 69
Sesostris, 94
Seti I, 25, 94
Seven Wonders of the World, 28, 73
shadoofs, 83
Sham an-Nasim, 65
Sinai Peninsula, 12, 13, 44, 47, 48, 90, 92, 93
Six-Day War, 12, 47
slaves, 10
Small Temple, 79
Sphinx, 32
sports, 60
St. Catherine's, 93
step pyramids, 28
Suez Canal, 11, 12, 13, 44, 45, 47, 94-97

Sweet Water Canal, 96
Syria, Syrians, 11, 40, 47, 70

T
temples, 24, 25, 31, 33, 79
Ten Commandments, 92
Thebes, 23, 24, 25, 33
Thutmoses, 23
tombs, 21, 22
trachoma, 87
Tunisia, 39
Tura, 29
Turkey, Turks, 12, 41, 69, 70
Tutankhamen, 35-38

U
United Arab Republic, 12, 47
United Nations, 44
United States, 12, 13, 45, 72, 75, 77, 82, 96
Upper Egypt, 10, 16, 21

V
Valley of the Tombs of the Kings, 25, 33

W
wadis, 89
water buffalo, 84, 85-86
water wheels, 84
Western Desert, 89, 91

Z
Zagazig, 96